A LITTLE BIT OF ME FO[R]

BY
MARK NICHOLAS

To Alison

Best Wishes

Mark Nicholas

The following pages contain poems that were written between 2003 and 2008 under my website name of minstrel-online which is now closed. After many requests by friends, I have decided to publish them so that others may read and hopefully enjoy them. Many people believe that these poems reflect me, my thoughts, my feelings, my emotions, and my naughty boy ways.

I have reviewed and edited most, as well as rewritten some. I hope you enjoy reading the poems as much as I have enjoyed writing them. I hope this first book will be just one of many and I look forward to writing more.

Many thanks to Helen Moule for encouragement and guidance, also Amanda Weakford at BrightVA Typing Services for layout check and proofreading.

Thank you for purchasing this book.

Mark Nicholas

All Rights Reserved

No part of this book may be reproduced in any form, or stored in a recovery system, by means, including but not limited to electronic or digital transferal, mechanical, photocopying, recording or otherwise published without similar conditions being obligatory on the successive purchaser or purchasers.

COPYRIGHT

Copyright © 2020 Mark Nicholas

DEDICATION

To Linda Autino. Rest in peace, my friend. So sorry we never met in life.

CONTENTS

THE BRA AND THE SOCK
HELP ME LOVE AGAIN
BESIDES MY POOL
READY FOR LOVE
MILLY MAY
SEARCH YOUR SOUL
THE PIMPLE
THAT CREATURE CALLED ARIES
IN MY BUBBLE
GOODNIGHT, MY SLEEPY FRIEND
JUST SIMPLE WORDS
MERLIN'S SPECTACULAR SHOW
BREASTS
DREAM DINNER
CASTLE ON THE HILL
MOMMA'S ANGRY RAP
MONDAYS WITH YOU
YOU ARE THE ONLY ONE
THE COST OF LIVING
BOIL ON THE BOT
BEE BO BOB
BE HERE WITH ME TONIGHT
A DOG'S LIFE
DID I TELL YOU
I LOVE YOU
CHRISTMAS PAST
A TICKLE
THE GIRLS' NIGHT OUT
NAUGHTY BOYS' RAP
LONESOME BLUE

THE BRA AND THE SOCK

The bra and the sock were talking one day
Both had plenty to say
The bra was moaning of being tossed around
And feeling dizzy all day
The sock said that's fine but this life of mine
I can never see where I am going
And no one ever sees my best part
Because only the top half is showing
Well that might be so but I'm always on show
Said the bra and life is not grand
Every so often I'm suddenly ripped open
And rummaged around by a hand
They pull this way and pull that way
And oh! how it makes me shout
But I get my own back when they open the clasp
I snap back and give them a clout
Ha ha said the sock that sounds good to me
I get my own back as well,
I wait until wash day and hide in the corner
And then I give off a bad smell

HELP ME LOVE AGAIN

Do you see it in my eyes
Can you see the sorrow
Do you know what lays in store
When I awake tomorrow

A lonely space within my soul
An empty space within my bed
No one to say good morning to
No one to kiss my head

I was in love some years ago
Oh how I loved you so
They do say what you reap
Is from the seeds you sow

Whatever happened then to me
Am I to take the blame
Live my life forever more
Fearing pain again

You say to search my soul
See what lays within
Can that be so, do you think so
Is the answer there within

You tell me seek with the soul
Not with the heart or eyes
You say the eyes can be deceived
That the heart can tell me lies

They come, they go, they don't last long
With some I feel so sure
But every time it ends the same
I feel so insecure

I run and hide myself away
Convince myself I'm right
That the one whose gone was not the one
For me they were not right

Now I do not seek no more
I hide in my comfy hole
A life without the love of another
A body with no soul
But I am only human
With so much love to give
Can you show me the reason
Why I can't love and live
Maybe you are right
Search my soul and find the pain
Then I can see where I went wrong
To help me love again

Should that chance then come my way
If I can overcome the pain
I will remember your wise words
That helped me love again

BESIDE MY POOL

When I sit beside my pool I feel a sense of calm
Lillies in the water and perhaps a weeping palm
The gentle sound of water as it runs along its path
The birds they swoop and play and use it as a bath
The ripples from the fish as they feed on the food I bring
The flowers round the edge in the breeze they gently swing
And you, my love, beside me radiant in the sun
We started this together and it has been such fun
As our children played we could hear them shriek and scream
The skies above bright and blue, the grass deep rich green
The colours of the fish they glisten in the light
The surface turns a moody blue to reflect the moon at night
The people as they come and go pass comments on our pool
We see the envy in their eyes as they turn away and drool
But you see I have no garden nor a family to be seen
It is just a vison that I get when I start to dream

READY FOR LOVE

I try to hide my feelings by keeping them inside
Only letting them out when I can safely hide
Now the time has come and I have to let them out
Been through all the torture and now I need to shout

You walked into my life when I was feeling down
I met you on a night when I had gone to town
No one in my life, I was happy on my own
Now you are the greatest that I have ever known

I was unsure at first where this relationship would go
The hurt I felt from the past I did not want to show
Slowly with your patience you made me tell it all
Now my heart tells me in love with you I'll fall

The past I can't forget, it haunts me every night
Many times I cannot sleep and with my mind I fight
Then when we are together you soothe away my fears
With you I feel so secure, I don't shed any tears

As we grow much closer now I wonder if you know
Just how much you mean to me I find it hard to show
Now I am ready to tell you the feelings in my heart
If it's me your looking for I'm ready for that start

All I ask of you is you take me as you see
Please understand that there is hurt deep in me
Treat me very gently, please my heart don't burn
I will give you the love you seek, for your love in return

MILLY MAY

Milly May went out one day
Never to go back home
Instead she kept on walking
Far away from home

She walked for many days
And slept out in the night
Had nature as her companion
At night the moon her light

As she walked the birds they sang
Making sweet music with their wings
She learnt to understand them
They told of many things

How they feared for their future
As man destroyed the land
They swooped and flew around her
And fed from her open hand

Then she met some otters
Who were playing in a stream
She sat down and she listened
Whilst they told her of their dream

To have a healthy river
Clean and full of fish
And not polluted by man's waste
Was their secret wish

Then down came a herd of deer
At the water's edge to drink
They said to Milly May
Oh! why can't man just think

Every day he plunders
And takes from nature's bank
Never putting back the things
Like wood that made the plank

She listened to their worries
And made them all a vow
That she would end their sorrow
She'd find a way somehow

And as she walked on further
More animals she did meet
She decided to share their nature
And kicked the shoes from off her feet

She ate only vegetation
And left some for others' use
For now Milly was a changed woman
For her past had no excuse

The animals kept up with her
And as she walked on more
The line of animals behind her
Was forty score and more

And when she finally found some land
She thought of a good use
A place where animals and man together
Could live in peaceful truce

And even though that Milly May
Has long since passed away
The legacy of what she did
Is still there to this day

A place for man and animals
To live safely side by side
A place that Milly started
And stayed until she died

So the next time you're out walking
And you stop to see the view
Remember that what you can see
Was created by the few

The few who were like Milly
Who chose to change her ways
So that animals and man together
Can share their future days

SEARCH YOUR SOUL

When your soul is lonely
Your heart is cold and blue
Life has lost its meaning
There's nothing there for you
Your soul has lost belief
Your heart has lost desire
No longer told you are the one
Who sets their passions on fire
Made to feel unwanted
Or wanted just for lust
Their needs for you external
Your soul is not a must
When you question what you want in life
And the answer cannot find
Do you really know just what you want
Is it written in your mind
Do you look because they noticed
Are you attracted by their style
Does their wealth impress upon you
Do you like the way they smile
These things are just material
They do not make one whole
To know just what it is you want
You need to read your soul
Then when you have achieved this
Your life will now take seed
And you will have the vision
For someone's soul to read
The truth is there within you
If you search it will come through
Then in life you will be able
To find the soul for you
A soul you never imagined
So different from the rest
A soul for life, a love for life
That soul will give you zest

THE PIMPLE

Ah ha! said the skin, I can feel you within
You are starting to make me go itchy
And though you are small I can't see you at all
My nerve ends are going all twitchy
But when you go red and you show your big head
I'll take out my tweezers to you
So you just keep growing, your head you start showing
And then I will get rid of you
For such a small spot you hurt me a lot
I hate it each time that you come
But the most painful time that I can recall
Is when you appear on my bum

THAT CREATURE CALLED ARIES

I saw her there with her golden hair
Her eyes of brown transfixed me to stare
I felt myself taken into her soul
I wanted her total, I wanted her whole

The passion I felt as we both kissed
Told me it was something she had missed
Her lips felt so soft they tasted like sweet wine
Emotions running wild as she pressed them on to mine

She told things in her own strange way
Which told of words she could not say
They told me through the way she kissed
Of the things in life that she had missed

My love for her grew stronger every single day
I did not doubt her motives and believed what she would say
The closeness seemed at times as if we were both as one
Then in a flash she disappeared suddenly she was gone

This creature I had brought alive had used me to be free
This Aries creature had struck again and this time it was me
And now free to wonder she will let you take her whole
Beware of his creature, Aries, for she will take away your soul

IN MY BUBBLE

I hide myself in here
Alone in my bubble
I know I will be safe in here
Free from any trouble
Here I can be revealing
Show my feelings without fear
For in my little bubble
Emotions stay well clear
And as the people pass on by
I can smile and laugh and flirt
For in my bubble I feel so safe
Knowing I won't be hurt

GOODNIGHT, MY SLEEPY FRIEND

Goodnight, goodnight, my sleepy friend
Time to go to bed
To lay your weary body down
And snuggle up in bed
Forget all your worries
Forget your deepest fears
A place snug and safe for you
Where you will shed no tears

Goodnight, goodnight, my sleepy friend
Lay down your weary head
Close your eyes and snuggle up
And dream whilst in your bed
Dream about your handsome prince
Who visits you at night
Or maybe in your dreams you see
A gallant handsome knight

Goodnight, goodnight, my sleepy friend
You are now in a trance
Perhaps with your handsome prince
You are going to a dance
You could be sailing on the sea
Or riding a horse and carriage
Maybe to a royal ball
Or maybe to a marriage

Goodnight, goodnight, my sleepy friend
The night is growing cold
Maybe you are snuggled up
With your knight so bold
Does he hold you in his powerful arms
For a journey through the sky
The gallant knight for whom you love
And for you that he would die

Goodnight, goodnight, my sleepy friend
And dream of a journey long
Where there is peace and beauty
And birds fill the air with song
Your knight will hold you close
He will not let you go
And there before your very eyes
Your future he will show

Goodnight, goodnight, my sleepy friend
You are now deep in sleep
With the gallant handsome knight
His promise he will keep
To guard your very soul
From feeling hurt again
To show you love you've never known
And rid you of your pain

Goodnight, goodnight, my sleepy friend
And snuggle up to me
I am that gallant handsome knight
The knight you wish to see
For in the morning when you wake
On the pillow you will find
A memory from the night before
That you dreamt in your mind

JUST SIMPLE WORDS

Sometimes I find it hard to use
The words you want to hear
I know just what I want to say
Then get overcome by fear
To know I hurt your feelings
I suppose sorry would be a start
But please believe me when I say
You are there in my heart
Just give me time to accept
Let me change and feel my way
For you are always on my mind
Every single day

MERLIN'S SPECTACULAR SHOW

Higgledee piggledee poggledee dee
Merlin has a show for thee
A show that will shock, a show that will thrill
Where he'll turn a dead rat into a ten dollar bill
And in the great hall hanging from bars
Rows and rows of dead frogs in jars
The sight of his tricks will drive you insane
With the thrill of it all you will come back again

Higgledee piggledee poggledee dee
With a wave of his wand you are in ecstasy
Where the dogs go meow and the cats go bow wow
And a triangle fits in a square hole somehow
With a flick of his wrist and a wave of his wand
All the fish will jump out of the pond
Where the birds do not sing and fly upside down
While a three-headed lizard pops up from his gown

Higgledee piggledee poggledee dee
If you think that is shocking there is still more to see
Like cows and goats hopping like frogs
And three-legged chickens dancing in clogs
Where you can go for a ride in his time machine
To a place where the sky is always bright green
In a land where all trees can sing and clap
And an ostrich will greet you wearing a hat

Higgledee piggledee poggledee dee
There is plenty of room and still more to see
With a flash and a bang and a wave of his hand
Your eyes will drop out and your head fill with sand
Where you look in a mirror and see nothing there
Then look again and you are covered in hair
With another flash bang and a wave from him
Your blood will pour out from a hole in your chin

Higgledee piggledee poggledee dee
Another trick over and yet more to see
Where cyber and space do not meet in the middle
And all things in life are just a big riddle
Where two plus two equals five
And all the dead are really alive
Water flows backwards and apples are pears
And wheels are not round but made up in squares

Higgledee piggledee poggledee dee
You will be amazed at what you see
Bishops and priests hanging in rows
And naked maidens exchanging blows
Where you see what you see is not one but another
Your brother is your sister and she is your mother
What you see at the show I think you will find
Is what Merlin sees deep in your mind

BREASTS

Breasts are such wonderful things
They really are a delight
There in the morning to stare at while yawning
And there for my pleasure at night
The large ones are wobbly and bounce up and down
And sometimes together they fight
But the small ones are best they just lie at rest
And oh! what a wonderful sight
Some breasts are pointed whilst others are round
Some even sag down like sacks
And some when you lay nature's laws disobey
And end up tucked under your backs
Then some can be hard whilst others are firm
And others are soft just like cream
But to see such nice boobs strapped in those boob tubes
Just makes me stand still and I dream
I sometimes get caught by the owners of some
They see me having a leer
I bet if they could and I know that they would
Give me a clip on the ear
But then some just smile and give me a grin
And they flirt as they walk past my side
With blouse buttons undone and the cups overrun
And a cleavage about a mile wide
So come on, you girls, show us some more
And dress them up just for the boys
I can assure you that they are a wonderful view
And much better than any old toys

DREAM DINNER

What could be more special than dinner for two
Holding hands at a table and gazing at you
To look deep in your eyes and know that you're whole
Hearing your words come from a beautiful soul
Then after hold hands on a blue moonlit beach
With the noise of the sea making its speech
And the stars up above seem to dance in the night
With you beside me a most beautiful sight
The breeze from the sea smells so fresh and so clear
With the smell of perfume as I nibble your ear
A sweet strawberry taste as your lips press on mine
The night as perfect as the finest red wine
But then as I look down at my desert with ice cream
I suddenly wake from my incredible dream
The waitress is telling her friend on the phone
We are not busy just a bloke sat on his own
I put on my coat and I leave her a tip
Then suddenly for some reason I lick my lip
And again you are there I am not alone
I am back in my dream to walk you back home

CASTLE ON THE HILL

Oh castle high upon the hill
Tell me your secrets if you will
How many years have you stood there
An empty shell, your walls are bare

Oh castle high upon the hill
Where once many dined and wine would spill
How many Kings and Queens have been
How many battles have you seen

Oh castle high upon the hill
Let me imagine if you will
When once you stood so proud and tall
To hear at night the Kingdoms call

Oh castle high upon the hill
Do tell your tales, do let them spill
Of days gone by and nights of old
Where knights in armour were so bold

Oh castle high upon the hill
You stand in mist and in the chill
Tell me was it warm inside
When all were by the fireside

Oh castle high upon the hill
For me it would be such a thrill
To venture back in time gone by
And see from your windows the night sky

Oh castle high upon the hill
Do me a favour, if you will
Send me a vision of how you looked
Where people lived and where they cooked

Oh castle high upon the hill
Your vision it was such a thrill
For I have been and I have seen
I saw it last night in my dream

MOMMA'S ANGRY RAP

Hey, you little creep, sit still while momma talks to you
Look me in the eye and don't that gum you chew
You gotta have manners to get on in this life
How do think you're ever gonna find yourself a wife
If you slope about all day and don't get any work
Everyone will say here comes that lazy jerk
He don't like work and don't look for none
All the friends he ever had have all got up and gone
The girls will walk away when they hear you say
Buy me a drink, babe, until I get some pay
And just look at your hair, do you not even care
What people might think, do you want them to stare
You look like trash and you got a bad rash
You can't afford clothes cos you ain't no cash
I gave you some last week and what did you do
Bought twenty ciggies and had a drink or two
You're just so mean, you ain't got no respect
You can't even talk in a proper dialect
And just look at your room, it's a darn disgrace
I walked in yesterday and got a dirty face
You don't help me to clean, you let me do it all
All you want to do is play with your football
It's kick it here, kick it there, kick it everywhere
Up against the wall or the table or the chair
I mean just for once could you notice that I'm here
Then you will understand why I sometimes shed a tear
All I want for you is to have a good life
Get a good job and meet a nice wife
I'm entitled to think and say the things I do
Cos for the last twenty years I have paid for you
So just for this once do something for me
Go and make your momma a nice cup of tea
Then when I've had a rest and built up my strength
You can come outside with me and help repair the fence
Then after that, before the sun goes down
You can go and get a brush and paint the woodwork brown
Then when you've done all that I've got a little job
Cleaning up the oven where you messed up the hob
And if it's not too late then you can take up the vac

Give your room a clean and put your clothes back on the rack
And any dirty washing you bring down to me
Tomorrow you will learn how to do the laundry
Then when you're tired from the work and feel like a sleep
I'm gonna play my music loud like you do, you little creep
Then maybe you will understand what living's all about
And get up off your idle bum and give yourself a clout
Get up early in the morning and go with your Uncle Bob
And don't come back into this house until you've got a job

MONDAYS WITH YOU

I've just spent two days with you
We had ourselves a ball
But now you have got to leave
And I'm heading for a fall
Tomorrow will be Monday
So I'll be feeling blue
How I wish that just for once
I could spend Mondays with you

Tuesday's not that good either
I'm still feeling blue
But three more days to go and then
I'll be seeing you
Wednesday it gets better
I think what we will do
How I wish that just for once
I could spend Mondays with you

Well Wednesday it just drags on by
I think all day of you
Then Thursday comes and I perk up
And I stop feeling blue
It's only one more day now
Till I'll be seeing you
How I wish that just for once
I could spend Mondays with you

Now Thursday's over quickly
I rush around all day
Only one more day to go
To hear the words you'll say
But then as I reach Friday
I know time will fly with you
How I wish that just for once
I could spend Mondays with you

Then Friday hits me like a bomb
Not long until tonight
When you step off that big red bus
You will look a beautiful sight
I'll hold you in my arms, squeezing you so tight
No longer missing you, I'll stop feeling blue
How I wish that just for once
I could spend Mondays with you

Now the weekend's over
I had such fun with you
But once again that time has come
For me to feel all blue
Just one more day I'd ask for
To be alone with you
How I wish that just for once
I could spend Mondays with you

YOU ARE THE ONLY ONE

If you could feel the pain I have
For the things I have just done
Then maybe you could understand
Why you are the only one
To lose you now would be such loss
Life would be misery
Please let me hear those words again
To say that you love me

THE COST OF LIVING

There it is behind the door,
Lying there upon the floor,
Every day another bill,
Just one more thing to make me ill,
We want it now or by this date,
All these bills I really hate,
And don't forget the generous loan,
The one the bank sold on the phone,
Then car tax, petrol, service too,
The daughter's school trip to the zoo,
New trainers for the eldest son,
So he can play out in the sun,
At least that's cheap and don't cost much,
Until you see the hole in his crutch,
Now new jeans, they have to be Lee,
Them kids think money grows on a tree,
The TV rental and licence need paying,
And another hour both the kids will be saying,
Can I have a fiver, can I have ten,
And for school next week I need a new pen,
The wife has just gone shopping,
Only God knows what she'll spend,
And her sister's going with her and she's always on the lend,
My shoes have holes, my feet are always wet,
And now the dog is limping so it's a trip to the vet,
The milkman's due and so is the rent,
Think that I will bugger off and just live in a tent.

BOIL ON THE BOT

Now the boil on the bot is more than a spot,
It's purple and larger in size,
If you give it a squeeze you let out a wheeze,
And tears stream down from your eyes.

It's really no fun when it's there on your bum,
You can't sit down nor can you stand,
The last thing you need is a good friend indeed,
Slapping your butt with their hand.

It gets knocked about and it does make you shout,
You have not got a clue what to do,
And to make things worse and that's when you curse,
Is when you sit down on the loo.

At night in your bed when you lay down your head,
That boil it throbs all night long,
But at least there's some ease and one can feel pleased,
That you decided to buy that new thong.

But then in the morn when you wake with the dawn,
And forget that you're cursed with the sod,
You roll on your side and your eyes open wide,
Cos you've given the darn thing a prod

BEE BO BOB

Here is the tale of Bee Bo Bob
Could not find himself a job
Every day, out he would go
And to employers his CV would show
Some would say no not today
Whilst others would just say go away
Up and down the streets he trudged
Feeling blue for being misjudged
Why would they not employ poor Bob
All he wanted was a job
Just a job to earn his keep
To afford a place where he could sleep
A room, a bed, a cooker and fire
He put out an ad saying man for hire
But all he got was no work here
Why not try again next year
In desperation he had a shot
At trying to win the lottery jackpot
He put on his last pound and made a wish
And gave his ticket a wishful kiss
Then on Saturday night his luck came in
Lucky Bob, he got his win
So now he looks for work no more
Instead he employs by the score
And when a beggar comes in sight
He takes him in for just one night
And next day gives the beggar a job
Remembering how hard it was, that's our Bee Bo Bob

BE HERE WITH ME TONIGHT

How I wish you were this doll
Then I could hold you tight
To talk with you and kiss with you
Throughout the darkest night
To feel your gentle fingers
Running up and down my spine
To know that I am truly yours
And know that you are mine

To feel your breath upon my face
As you soothe away my fears
And feel you gently stroke my hair
As you wipe away my tears
For I have been alone now
For so long it's hard to know
I long to have you in my arms
My love for you I'll show

To laugh with you and cry with you
To hold you oh so tight
Our souls both united
As we sleep together this night
And in the early hours
When the day begins to break
To know that you with gentle care
My body and soul will take

And we together will both be as one
As our bodies both entwine
Our souls both united
A feeling so divine
But this cannot be so
For I know not where you are
Please, where are you my lover
Are you near to me or far

So for now my doll will have to do
I can call it what I like
Tom, Dick, Harry
Martin, Jack or Mike
I know that you are out there
Please come and find my soul
And I will give you all my love
If you give yourself whole

A DOG'S LIFE

I am in serious trouble for I have done a poo
When dad gets hold of me he will smack me with his shoe
But it's not all my fault I have not had a walk
Cos he's been on the phone all day and all he's done is talk

I tapped him on the knee I scratched at the door
I scratched so much that now I have a splinter in my paw
What must a dog just have to do to get it through to you
That just like you we need a loo because we need a poo

DID I TELL YOU

Did I tell you I was sorry
Did I say that I was sad
Did I hug you in the kitchen
Even though you made me mad
Did I tell you that I loved you
Did I say you're the only one
Did I tell you that I need you
That life with you is fun
Did I really say those nasty things
Did I really make you cry
Did I not listen when you told me
Now I sit and wonder why
Did I not realise you were leaving
Did I not see it in your eyes
Did I not see the hurt I caused you
By telling all those lies
Did I know you were unhappy
Did I know you hated me
Did I know you had found another
Someone who's not like me

I LOVE YOU

Why is it that I love you so
Well these words will let you know
I love you because you are so kind
The gentlest heart that I could find
Someone in whom my trust is whole
Who I can love with all my soul
To be my strength when I am weak
And comfort me if I should weep
Someone who cares for me each day
There to listen to what I say
To be there when I need a hug
Be my nurse when I've a bug
Does not shout when I am mad
But understands when I am sad
To share with me my hopes and fears
Be there to gently wipe my tears
But most of all why I love you
Is simply because you are you

CHRISTMAS PAST

Christmas day has come and gone
The goose was not that fat
I got a pair of socks
Granny got a hat
The jelly in the trifle
It did not even wobble
The granddaughter she cried all day
With her hair caught in a bobble
The toys they needed batteries
The shops they were all shut
Grandad for forgetting them
Got kicked by grandma in the butt
So here is looking for New Year
I hope it will be right
As I have just bought every battery
I could see in sight

A TICKLE

A tickle in the morning
A tickle in the night
A tickle just behind the ear
A tickle where it's right
A tickle when you are fully clothed
A tickle when you are bare
A tickle from someone you know
A tickle that says I care
A tickle when you are feeling down
A tickle when you are sad
A tickle from a loving mum
A tickle from a dad
A tickle from someone you love
A tickle from one you don't
A tickle from your very best friend
A tickle from one remote
A tickle from your enemy
A tickle will cause a cease
A tickle will go a long long way
A tickle for world peace

THE GIRLS' NIGHT OUT

Lotty, Dotty, Motty and Totty
All went out for a night
They went out to dine and had some nice wine
And ended up on Diamond White

Lotty and Totty got a bit blotty
While Motty got out of her head
And as for poor Dotty her face went all spotty
Turning a bright coloured red

Motty felt grotty and threw up on Dotty
And Totty and Lotty got ill
While Motty went potty for some guy called Scotty
And said if you want then I will

The night for poor Dotty got rather potty
And for Lotty it got even worse
While dancing with Totty a hand fondled her botty
And ended up stealing her purse

Now Motty dumped Scotty after they had got hottie
While Lotty and Dotty both copped
Lotty for Spotty and Dotty for Grotty
And off to the car park they hopped

Now Totty alone also wanted some bone
And looked round the bar for a hunk
While Lotty and Dotty with Spotty and Grotty
Were both having one hell of a bunk

A good-looking bloke felt he wanted a poke
And saw Totty looking at him
He gave her a smile and waited a while
Then gave her another big grin

She grinned back at him and extended her chin
And beckoned him by waving her bag
He said he was Jotty she said I am Totty
And how would you like a good shag

When Lotty and Dotty had humped Spotty and Grotty
They both went back into the bar
There they found Motty feeling a bloke's botty
And asking if he had a car

He said that he did and away they both slid
While Lotty and Dotty drank more
Then they saw Totty with that bloke called Jotty
Doing it there on the floor

When all was done and the girls had had fun
It was time to go home to their beds
Lotty and Dotty and Motty and Totty
The four all pissed out of their heads

NAUGHTY BOYS' RAP

I got me a girl, I'm all in a twirl
She don't know nothing and she's called Shirl
We went on a date, I got her home late
There was her father standing at the gate
He said hey boy she isn't no toy
Then put the dampers on me having some joy
So off home I went like a bad boy sent
And all I got was the smell of her scent
On the way home I found me a dog
He looked like he'd lost his way in the fog
I picked him up, he gave me a lick
And all the way home he chased me a stick
There at the door in a 4X4
Was a flash-looking geezer with the chick next door
He gave her chase, she slapped his face
And ran away from him saying give me some space
I said hey dude don't be so mean
Can't you see this girl likes to live clean
She looked at me and said with glee
A knight in shining armour I've got for me
Then we went in mine and drunk some wine
And woke up in the morning feeling just fine
But now I'm on the run cos I baked me a bun
And her daddy's after me with a big shot gun

LONESOME BLUE

When I am all alone in bed and I am feeling blue
I get out all my photos that I took of you
It seems sad to think what we were
Together all the time, soulmates for a year
Now we are apart we don't talk no more
I come home every night and see an empty floor
You took whatever we had, you took it all in whole
And when you left you took my heart, you even took my soul

Is there a way we can take back the terrible things we said
To wish we had not used those words and used our heads instead
My love for you was true, I thought it was so pure
I believed that for my broken soul you really were the cure
It felt oh so good being in your arms just like I thought it should
To feel you close to me, I never dreamt that you would
But now you have gone your way and I am missing you
A lonely soul in a hole feeling rather blue

So now I feel that my life is like an empty book
The pages turn each day but no one seems to look
I walk along the street where we used to meet at night
I think I see you sometimes, is that really you in sight
But life at times is so unkind when it plays tricks with your head
I try to hide from the truth and often go to bed
But that is when I feel alone and start to think of you
A lonely soul on my own just a lonesome blue

Printed in Great Britain
by Amazon